Oxford First Thesaurus

Bestselling first thesaurus

new edition

Compiled by Andrew Delahunty

OXFORD
UNIVERSITY PRESS

OXFORD
UNIVERSITY PRESS

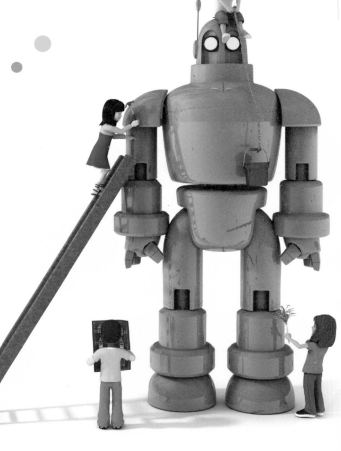

Great Clarendon Street, Oxford OX2 6DP

Oxford University Press is a department of the University of Oxford.
It furthers the University's objective of excellence in research,
scholarship, and education by publishing worldwide in

Oxford   New York

Auckland   Cape Town   Dar es Salaam   Hong Kong   Karachi
Kuala Lumpur   Madrid   Melbourne   Mexico City   Nairobi
New Delhi   Shanghai   Taipei   Toronto

With offices in

Argentina   Austria   Brazil   Chile   Czech Republic   France   Greece
Guatemala   Hungary   Italy   Japan   Poland   Portugal   Singapore
South Korea   Switzerland   Thailand   Turkey   Ukraine   Vietnam

Oxford is a registered trade mark of Oxford University Press
in the UK and in certain other countries

© Oxford University Press 2012

Database right Oxford University Press (maker)

First published 2012

Artwork by Dynamo Limited

British Library Cataloguing in Publication Data
Data available

ISBN: 978 0 19 275683 1 (hardback)
ISBN: 978 0 19 275684 8 (paperback)
423.1
10 9 8 7 6 5 4 3 2 1

Printed in Malaysia

TEACHERS
For inspirational support plus
free resources and eBooks
www.oxfordprimary.co.uk

PARENTS
Help your child's reading
with essential tips, phonics
support and free eBooks
www.oxfordowl.co.uk

Introduction

The **Oxford First Thesaurus** helps you discover lots of different words you can use in your own writing. It helps you to choose just the right word for what you want to say or write. It also helps you to try using new and different words rather than using the same ones all the time.

Making your writing more interesting

Imagine you are writing about what you did at the weekend.
You might start like this:

> I had a nice day on Saturday. The weather was nice so we went to a nature park. The lady who showed us round was very nice. We saw lots of nice animals, including some deer. I had a nice chocolate ice cream.

Can you see how the word **nice** is used over and over again? It would be more interesting if you sometimes used another word instead. If you look up **nice** in this thesaurus you will find other words you can choose which have a similar meaning.
So you could write this instead:

> I had an enjoyable day on Saturday. The weather was fine so we went to a nature park. The lady who showed us round was very friendly. We saw lots of nice animals, including some deer. I had a delicious chocolate ice cream.

What is a thesaurus?

A thesaurus is a book of words. It puts together words that have a similar meaning. A thesaurus is not the same as a dictionary. A dictionary tells you what a lot of different words mean. A thesaurus helps you find other words with the same meaning.

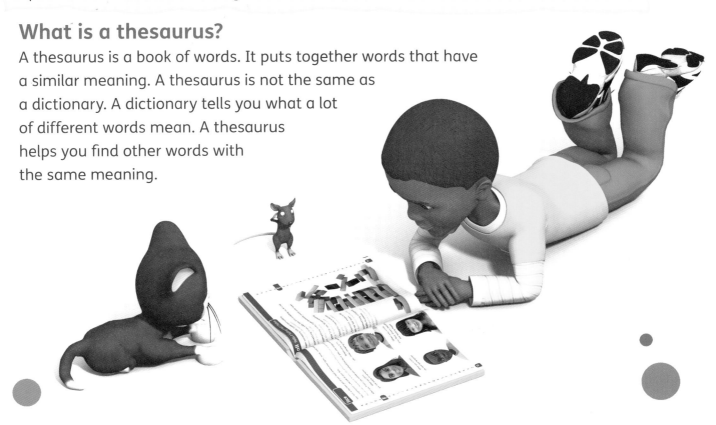

Introduction

headwords

The word at the top of each page is called the **headword**. It is the starting point for finding other useful words. The headwords are arranged in alphabetical order. The **alphabet** appears at the side of the page to help you.

synonyms

The **synonyms** are the words in thick blue text. These are words that are close in meaning to the headword. If you look at the headword **soft**, you can see that the words **fluffy, floppy**, and **squashy** all have meanings similar to **soft**. At the page for **eat**, you will find other words that you can use to talk about different ways of eating, such as **bite, chew, gobble, munch, nibble**, and **gnaw**.

definitions

Definitions tell you what words mean. They are often given for the headwords. Definitions are also given for many of the synonyms to help you choose the right word for what you want to say or write. The definition for fluffy tells you that something that is **fluffy** has soft hair, fur, or feathers.

example sentences

Example sentences show you how to use the word in a sentence. The example sentence for **fluffy** is A fluffy yellow chick hopped out.

opposites

With some words, there is another word that means the **opposite**. You can sometimes find these at the bottom of the page. If you look at the bottom of the page that has the headword **soft**, you can see that its opposite is **hard**.

Other useful words

On some pages you will find words that are useful if you are talking or writing about the headword. So at the page for **water**, you will find words such as **flow, pour, splash, drop**, and **trickle**. At the page for **space**, you will find words like **spacecraft, astronaut, moon**, and **planet**.

Some entries list different kinds of a particular thing. So at the page for **book**, you will find words for different kinds of books, like **atlas, diary, dictionary**, and **encyclopedia**.

Index

If you want to find a word quickly in the thesaurus try looking in the **Index** at the back. This lists all the words in alphabetical order and tells you on what page you can find each word.

Introduction

These are the main features in the thesaurus:

headword

definition

example sentence

alphabet

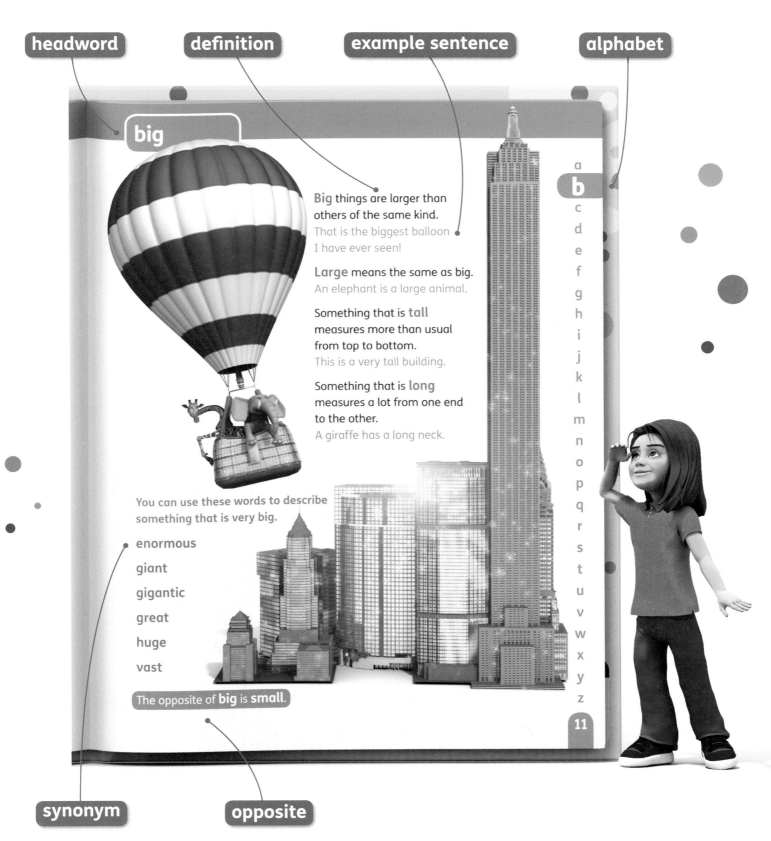

big

Big things are larger than others of the same kind.
That is the biggest balloon I have ever seen!

Large means the same as big.
An elephant is a large animal.

Something that is **tall** measures more than usual from top to bottom.
This is a very tall building.

Something that is **long** measures a lot from one end to the other.
A giraffe has a long neck.

You can use these words to describe something that is very big.

enormous

giant

gigantic

great

huge

vast

The opposite of **big** is **small**.

a
b
c
d
e
f
g
h
i
j
k
l
m
n
o
p
q
r
s
t
u
v
w
x
y
z

11

synonym

opposite

angry

If someone is **angry**, they are not pleased at all with what someone has done or said.
Cinderella's stepmother was so angry she stamped her feet.

You can also say that they are **annoyed** or **cross**.
Cinderella's sisters were cross with her all the time.

If someone is **furious** or **in a rage**, they are very angry.
The ugly sisters came home in a rage.

If someone **loses their temper**, they become angry all of a sudden.

Someone who is **bad-tempered** or **grumpy** is often in a bad mood.
Why are you so grumpy today?

animal

These are all different animals.

bear   bird   camel   cat   deer   dog

elephant   giraffe   hippo   horse   kangaroo

lion   mouse   rabbit   tiger

bad

Bad is a very common word and it has a lot of different meanings.

You can often use another word instead.

The bad queen hated Snow White.
You could say **wicked** instead.

The apple had a very bad smell.
You could say **nasty** or **revolting** or **horrible** instead.

What a bad dog!
You could say **naughty** instead.

I feel bad about forgetting his birthday.
You could say **awful** or **dreadful** or **terrible** instead.

She is bad at spelling.
You could say **poor** instead.

SnoWite

The opposite of **bad** is **good**.

beautiful

You say someone or something is **beautiful** if you enjoy looking at them or listening to them.
What a beautiful rainbow!

Here are some other words you can use.

lovely
Snow White sang a lovely song.

pretty
She wore a pretty dress.

handsome
A handsome prince listened to her singing.

sweet
'What a sweet voice!' he said.

bend bends / bending / bent

If you **bend** something, you change its shape so it is not straight any more.

The children are good at bending balloons into animal shapes.

If something **curves**, it bends round smoothly.

The swan's neck curves gently.

If something **turns**, it changes direction.

The bus turns left at the top of the road.

If you **twist** something, you bend or turn it.

Lucy can make a dog by twisting balloons.

If something **twists** or **winds**, it keeps changing direction.

The road twists and turns between the hills.

To **zigzag** means to move from one side to the other with sharp turns.

Jake's balloon zigzagged through the air.

big

Big things are larger than others of the same kind.
That is the biggest balloon I have ever seen!

Large means the same as big.
An elephant is a large animal.

Something that is **tall** measures more than usual from top to bottom.
This is a very tall building.

Something that is **long** measures a lot from one end to the other.
A giraffe has a long neck.

You can use these words to describe something that is very big.

enormous

giant

gigantic

great

huge

vast

The opposite of **big** is **small.**

bird

These are all different birds.

swan

budgerigar

magpie

eagle

owl

parrot

penguin

pelican

robin

pigeon

woodpecker

chicken

A **bit** of something is a small part of it.
The plate smashed to bits on the floor.

A **piece** of something is a part or bit of it.
Would you like a piece of cake?

Here are some words you can use to talk about bits of things.

a **slice** of bread

a **dollop** of jam

a **crumb** of
bread or cake

a **scrap** of cloth

a **lump** of sugar

A B C D E F G H I J K L M N O P Q R S T U V W X Y Z

Here are words for different books.

An **atlas** is a book of maps.

A **diary** is a book in which you can write down what happens each day.

A **dictionary** is a book where you can find out what a word means and how to spell it.

An **e-book** is a book that you can read on a screen.

An **encyclopedia** is a book or set of books containing information about lots of different things.

A **storybook** is a book full of stories.

A **thesaurus** is a book that gives you sets of words that all have a similar meaning.

brave

If you are **brave**, you show that you are not afraid.

The brave knight was reading a book on dragons.

These words also mean brave.

bold

courageous

daring

fearless

A
B
C
D
E
F
G
H
I
J
K
L
M
N
O
P
Q
R
S
T
U
V
W
X
Y
Z

If something breaks, it goes into pieces.
Careful, that mug will break if you drop it.

You can use these words to talk about different things breaking.

If something snaps, it breaks in two with a sharp noise.
My pencil has snapped.

If it splits, it breaks or tears open.
Your trousers have split at the back!

If it bursts, it breaks open suddenly.
The football burst so we had to stop playing.

If it pops, it breaks open with a bang.
First one balloon popped, then another.

If it cracks, it breaks so that there are thin lines on it but it does not come to pieces.
Look, the jug has started to crack.

If it smashes, it breaks into lots of pieces with a loud noise.
The mirror fell over and smashed on the ground.

A **bright** light shines strongly.
The moon is very bright tonight.

Shiny means very bright.
The treasure chest is full of shiny gold coins.

If something is **gleaming**, it shines with a soft light.

If something is **sparkling** or **glittering**, it shines with
a lot of tiny flashes of bright light, like diamonds do.

If something is **dazzling**, it is so bright that it hurts your eyes.
The car headlights were dazzling.

Bright colours are strong and easy to see.
The parrot has bright red and blue feathers.

Something that has a lot
of bright colours is **colourful**.
Jake's parrot is very colourful.

A
B
C
D
E
F
G
H
I
J
K
L
M
N
O
P
Q
R
S
T
U
V
W
X
Y
Z

When things **change**, they become different.
Caterpillars change into butterflies.

When something **turns** into something else, it changes.
The frog turned into a handsome prince.

You can also say that one thing **becomes** something else.
As the sun goes down, the blue sky becomes pink.

If you **switch** something, you change it and put something else in its place.
Do you mind if I switch channels?

If you **swap** something, you give it to someone in return for something else.
Can we swap seats so I can look out of the window?

When you **clean** something, you get all the dirt or stains off.

You can use these words to talk about different ways of cleaning.

You **brush** something with a hairbrush, toothbrush, or other kind of brush.

You **dust** something with a duster.

You **rinse** something in clean water.

You **scrub** something with a hard brush.

You **sweep** something with a broom.

You **wash** something with water and soap.

You **wipe** something with a cloth.

A
B
C
D
E
F
G
H
I
J
K
L
M
N
O
P
Q
R
S
T
U
V
W
X
Y
Z

Someone who is **clever** learns and understands things easily.

These words also mean clever.

bright

intelligent

brainy

Brilliant means very clever indeed.

Someone who is **wise** knows and understands many things.

Someone who is **cunning** is clever at tricking people.

clothes

These are all different kinds of clothes.

coat   dress   jacket   jumper   pyjamas   shirt

shorts   skirt   socks   sweatshirt   trousers

cold

If you are **cold**, you feel that you want to put on warm clothes, or stand near something warm.

The weather got very cold and it began to snow.

If something is **cool**, it feels quite cold.

Put the juice in the fridge to keep it cool.

These words also mean cold.

chilly It was a chilly day.

freezing Can we go back in? I'm freezing!

frozen Jake's fingers were frozen.

icy An icy wind was blowing.

The opposite of **cold** is **hot**.

colour

These are all different colours.

black   blue   **brown**   green   **grey**

orange   pink   **purple**   red

violet   white   yellow

23

A
B
C
D
E
F
G
H
I
J
K
L
M
N
O
P
Q
R
S
T
U
V
W
X
Y
Z

Here are some words you can use if you are talking or writing about your computer.

screen

disk

printer

mouse

keyboard

If you **cook** something, you get it ready to eat by heating it.

You can use these words to describe different ways of cooking.

When you **bake** something, you cook it in an oven. You can bake bread and cakes.

When you **boil** something, you cook it in boiling water.

When you **fry** something, you cook it in hot fat in a pan.

When you **grill** something, you cook it over or under a flame or heated surface.

When you **scramble** eggs, you cook them by mixing them up and heating them in a pan

When you **toast** something, you cook it by heating it under a grill or in a toaster.

A
B
C
D
E
F
G
H
I
J
K
L
M
N
O
P
Q
R
S
T
U
V
W
X
Y
Z

If you **cut** something, you use scissors or a knife.

Here are some words you can use for cutting different things.

You **carve** meat.

You **chop** wood
with an axe.

You **mow** the lawn.

You **saw** wood.

You can **trim** your hair.

You **slice** bread.

dirty

Something that is **dirty** is covered with mud, food, or other marks.
Sam came in from the garden with a dirty face.

Dusty means covered with dust.
These shelves are dusty.

Muddy means covered with mud.
Look at the muddy footprints all over the floor.

If something is **smudged**, it is marked with streaks of dirt.
The mirror is smudged.

These words mean very dirty.

filthy   grubby   mucky

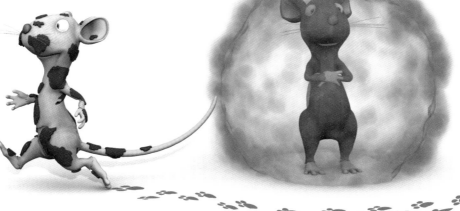

The opposite of **dirty** is **clean**.

A
B
C
D
E
F
G
H
I
J
K
L
M
N
O
P
Q
R
S
T
U
V
W
X
Y
Z

Do is a very common word and it has a lot of different meanings.

You can often use another word instead.

Sam said he would do paper planes for everyone.
You could say **make** instead.

Don't forget to do all your homework.
You could say **finish** instead.

Will five big sheets of paper do?
You could say **be enough** instead.

We are going to do air travel at school today.
You could say **learn about** instead.

If something is **easy**, you can do it or understand it without any trouble.
Paper planes are easy to make.

Simple means the same as easy.
Just follow these simple instructions.

If something is **clear**, it is easy to see, hear, or understand.
Speak in a clear voice.

If something is **obvious**, it is very easy to see or understand.
The answer to the riddle is obvious.

If something is **plain**, it is easy to see or understand.
It is plain to see Sam likes making things.

1.

2.

3.

4.

5.

6.

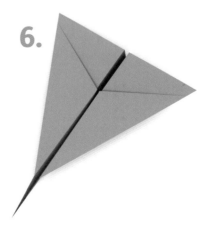

The opposite of **easy** is **hard** or **difficult**.

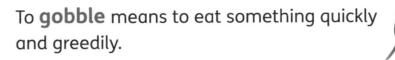

A
B
C
D
E
F
G
H
I
J
K
L
M
N
O
P
Q
R
S
T
U
V
W
X
Y
Z

When you **eat**, you take food into your mouth and swallow it.

You can use these words to talk about different ways of eating.

If you **bite** something, you use your teeth to cut into it.

When you **chew** food, you break it up between your teeth.

To **gobble** means to eat something quickly and greedily.

To **munch** means to chew something noisily.

To **nibble** means to take tiny bites.

To **taste** means to try a little bit of food to see what it is like.

These words are especially to do with animals.

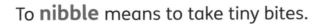

To **gnaw** means to keep biting something which is hard.
The dog gnawed the bone.

To **graze** means to eat grass.
Cows are grazing in the field.

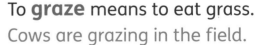

To **peck** means to eat something with a beak.
Hens pecked at the corn.

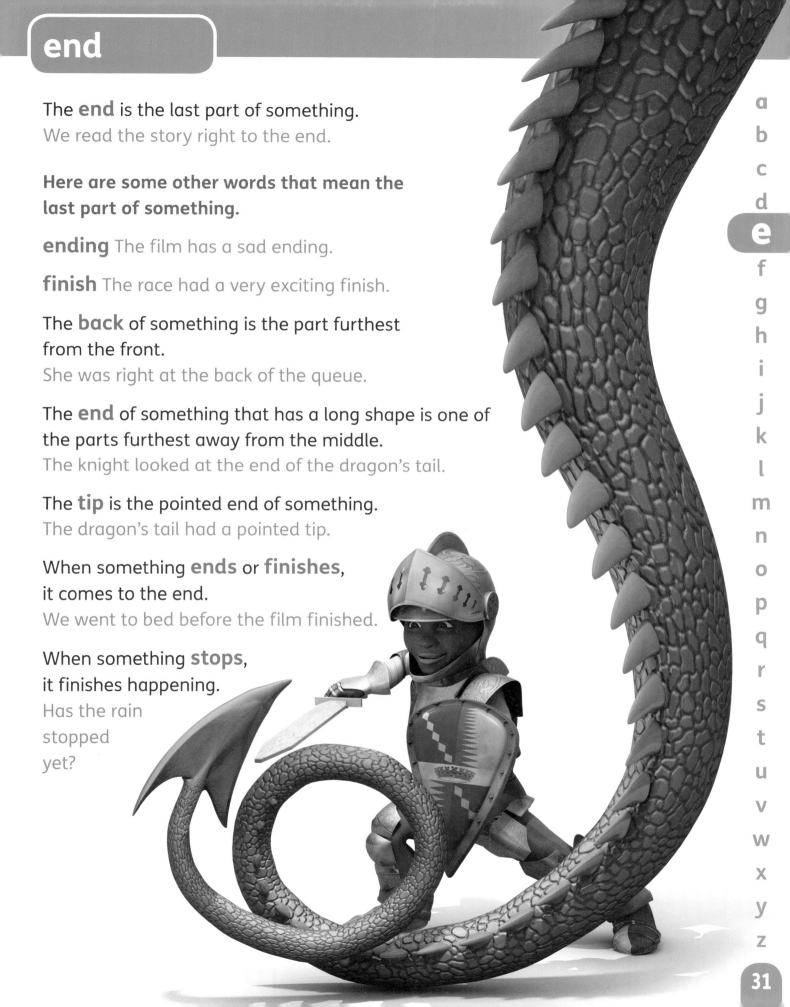

end

The **end** is the last part of something.
We read the story right to the end.

Here are some other words that mean the last part of something.

ending The film has a sad ending.

finish The race had a very exciting finish.

The **back** of something is the part furthest from the front.
She was right at the back of the queue.

The **end** of something that has a long shape is one of the parts furthest away from the middle.
The knight looked at the end of the dragon's tail.

The **tip** is the pointed end of something.
The dragon's tail had a pointed tip.

When something **ends** or **finishes**, it comes to the end.
We went to bed before the film finished.

When something **stops**, it finishes happening.
Has the rain stopped yet?

a b c d **e** f g h i j k l m n o p q r s t u v w x y z

face

Your **face** is the front part of your head where your eyes, nose, and mouth are.

Your **expression** is the look on your face.

You can use these words to describe different expressions on a person's face.

When you **frown**, you wrinkle your forehead because you are angry or worried.

When you **glare**,
you look angrily at someone.

When you **grin**,
you smile showing your teeth.

When you **scowl**,
you look bad-tempered.

When you **smile**, your face shows
that you are feeling happy.

When something **falls**, it comes down suddenly.
Leaves fall from the trees in autumn.

If something **drops**, it falls. If you **drop** something, you let it fall.
Don't drop the cake!

If something **sinks**, it goes downwards, usually under water.
The ship is sinking.

If you **trip**, you fall over something.
Lucy tripped over a rock.

To **topple** means to fall over.
That pile of blocks is about to topple.

To **tumble** means to fall over or fall down.
Jill tumbled down the hill.

If something **collapses**, it falls to pieces.
Miki pulled a block out and the whole tower collapsed.

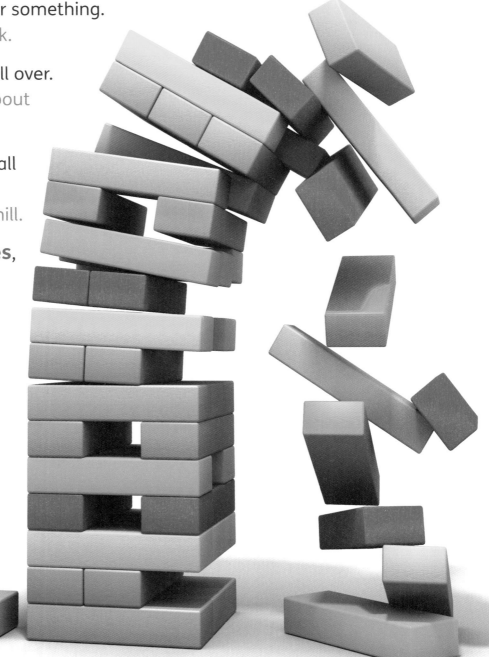

A
B
C
D
E
F
G
H
I
J
K
L
M
N
O
P
Q
R
S
T
U
V
W
X
Y
Z

Something that is **fast** moves quickly.

Jake is very fast on his bike. He can cycle very fast.

To be **quick** means to move or do something fast.

If we're quick, we'll be able to catch the bus.

Something **quick** does not take very long.

Can I have a quick look at your comic?

Something that is **swift** or **rapid** moves very quickly.

If you do something **quickly**, it does not take you long to do it.

We got dressed very quickly and ran downstairs.

Swiftly and **rapidly** mean the same as quickly.

When you **hurry**, you walk or run quickly, or try to do something quickly.

Let's hurry or we'll be late.

You **rush** or **dash** somewhere when you are in a hurry.

find finds / finding / found

When you **find** something that has been lost, you get it back.
Sam couldn't find his roller skates.

When you **discover** something, you find it.
The explorers discovered a golden statue in the jungle.

If you **spot** something, you notice it by looking hard for it.
See if you can spot the mouse.

If you **look for** something, you try to find it.
Miki looked for her friends all over the house.

When you **search** or **hunt**, you look very carefully for something.
I've searched everywhere for my red shoes, but I can't find them.

If you **seek** something, you try to find it.
Let's play hide and seek.

A
B
C
D
E
F
G
H
I
J
K
L
M
N
O
P
Q
R
S
T
U
V
W
X
Y
Z

Fire is the heat
and bright light that
comes from things that are burning.

A **flame** is one of the hot, bright strips of light
that rise up from a fire.

You also get **smoke**.

If something is **burning**, it is on fire.

A **fire** is something which keeps people warm.

There are different kinds such as a **coal fire**,
an **electric fire**, and a **gas fire**.

A **fireplace** is the part of a room
where the fire is.

A **bonfire** is a fire
which someone lights
outdoors.

fix

If you **fix** something that is broken, you make it useful again.
Jake is trying to fix his shield.

If you **mend** or **repair** something, you fix it.
He needs to mend his broken sword too.

If you **patch** something,
you put a piece of material on it to mend it.
Mum patched my jeans.

If you **sew**,
you use a needle and cotton.
Dad sewed the button
back on his shirt.

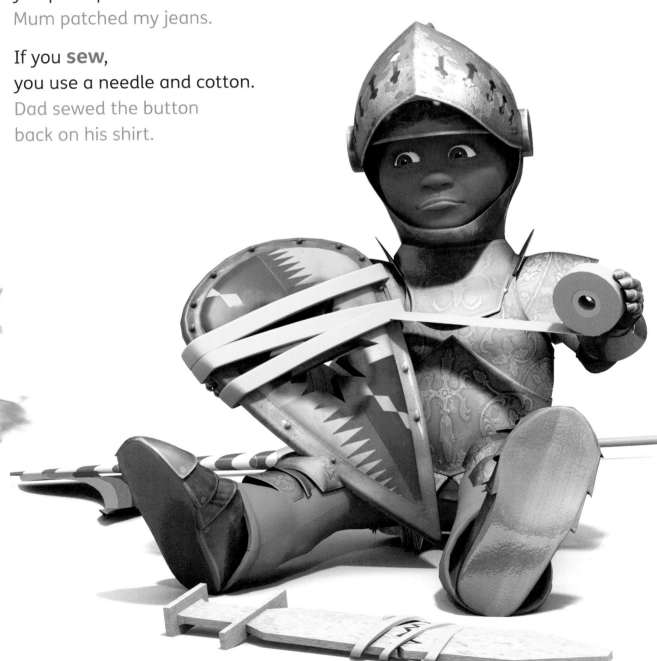

A
B
C
D
E
F
G
H
I
J
K
L
M
N
O
P
Q
R
S
T
U
V
W
X
Y
Z

When things **fly**, they move through the air.

When a bird or butterfly **flaps** its wings,
it moves them up and down or from side to side.

To **flutter** means to fly by flapping the wings quickly.
A butterfly fluttered in through the window.

When a bird **glides**, it flies smoothly
without flapping its wings.

When a plane **glides**, it flies without an engine.

If something **hovers**, it stays in one place in the air.

To **soar** means to fly high in the air.
The rocket soared into the sky.

To **swoop** means to fly down suddenly.
The eagle swooped down.

If a bird or aeroplane **takes off**,
it goes up into the air to begin flying.

Food is anything that you eat.

If you are **hungry**, you want something to eat.

A **meal** is the food you eat at different times of the day.

These are words for meals you can have.

A **snack** is a small meal.

You eat **breakfast** in the morning.

You eat **lunch** in the middle of the day.

You eat **dinner** as the main meal of the day.

You eat **tea** in the afternoon or early evening.

You eat **supper** as a meal or snack in the evening.

A **picnic** is a meal you eat in the open air.

A **feast** is a special meal for a lot of people.

Someone who is **frightened** or **scared** or **afraid** is worried that something bad might happen.
My brother is frightened of spiders.

Someone who is **terrified** is very frightened.

If something **frightens** a person or animal, it makes them feel afraid.
The ghost frightened Jake and Miki.

Scare means the same as frighten.

fruit

These are all different kinds of fruit.

apple

mango

banana

grapefruit

melon

peach

pineapple

raspberries

blackberries

apricot

cherries

lemon

pear

plum

orange

grapes

strawberries

A
B
C
D
E
F
G
H
I
J
K
L
M
N
O
P
Q
R
S
T
U
V
W
X
Y
Z

If something is **full**, there is no more room in it.

The jar is full of sweets.

If a place is full of people, you can say that it is **crowded** or **packed**.

The hall is packed.

If something is very full, you can say that it is **crammed** or **bursting**.

Get is a very common word and it has a lot of different meanings.

You can often use another word instead.

I hope I get a lot of birthday presents.
You could say **receive** instead.

Can we get some sweets
on the way home?
You could say **buy** instead.

Get your sister from the garden.
You could say **fetch** instead.

Grandma, will you get me from
school today?
You could say **collect** instead.

When did you get here?
You could say **arrive** instead.

Take a drink with you in case you
get thirsty.
You could say **become** instead.

a
b
c
d
e
f
g
h
i
j
k
l
m
n
o
p
q
r
s
t
u
v
w
x
y
z

43

give gives / giving / gave / given

If you **give** something to someone, you let them have it.

Jake likes to give presents.

If you **offer** something, you hold it out and ask someone if they would like it.

Sam went round the room, and offered everyone a piece of cake.

If you **hand** something to someone, you give it to them with your hand.

Will you hand me the phone?

If you **pass** something, you hand it over to someone.

Please pass the butter.

If you **lend** something of yours to someone, you let them have it for a short time.

Lucy is happy to lend me her watch.

A **present** is something you give to someone.

The opposite of **give** is **take**.

Go is a very common word and it has a lot of different meanings.

You can often use another word instead.

The children sing a song as they go down the lane.
You could say **walk** instead.

A racing car can go very fast.
You could say **travel** instead.

Is it time to go?
You could say **leave** instead.

Does this path go to the waterfall?
You could say **lead** instead.

Where did my bike go to?
You could say **disappear** instead.

My stopwatch won't go.
You could say **work** instead.

Where do these coats go?
You could say **belong** instead.

Where does this piece go in the jigsaw?
You could say **fit** instead.

Put the milk in the fridge or it will go sour.
You could say **become** instead.

a
b
c
d
e
f
g
h
i
j
k
l
m
n
o
p
q
r
s
t
u
v
w
x
y
z

good

Good is a very common word and it has a lot of different meanings.

You can often use another word instead.

This is a good book.
You could say **enjoyable** instead.

Be a good boy.
You could say **well-behaved** instead.

He was a good king.
You could say **kind** or **nice** instead.

There's a good smell coming from the oven.
You could say **nice** or **lovely** or **fine** instead.

This work is good.
You could say **well done** instead.

The opposite of **good** is **bad**.

happy

When you are **happy**, you feel pleased about something, or like things the way they are.

The king looked really happy when he saw the wonderful feast.

These other words also mean happy.

cheerful Lucy is always cheerful.

jolly The baker had a very jolly laugh.

merry Old King Cole was a merry old soul.

glad I'm glad you could come to my party.

pleased Sam was very pleased with all his presents.

The opposite of **happy** is **sad**.

a
b
c
d
e
f
g
h
i
j
k
l
m
n
o
p
q
r
s
t
u
v
w
x
y
z

47

A
B
C
D
E
F
G
H
I
J
K
L
M
N
O
P
Q
R
S
T
U
V
W
X
Y
Z

Something that is **hard** is not easy to cut or scratch.
Goldilocks said 'This bed is too hard'.

Something that is **stiff** is not easily bent.
You will need some stiff cardboard.

Something that is **solid** does not go in when you press it and does not have air in it.
The concrete is completely solid now.

When something **sets**, it becomes stiff or hard.
The jelly hasn't set yet.

The opposite of this meaning of **hard** is **soft**.

Things that are **hard** to do are not easy and need a lot of effort.
These sums are too hard.

Difficult means the same as hard.
Sam was trying to do a difficult jigsaw puzzle.

The opposite of this meaning of **hard** is **easy**.

have has / having / had

Have is a very common word and it has a lot of different meanings.

You can often use another word instead.

I have lots of books about wizards and witches.
You could say **own** instead.

I like books that have pictures in them.
You could say **contain** instead.

Did you have some nice birthday presents?
You could say **receive** or **get** instead.

I have to find the missing pieces.
You could say **need to** or **must** instead.

A
B
C
D
E
F
G
H
I
J
K
L
M
N
O
P
Q
R
S
T
U
V
W
X
Y
Z

If you **hit** something, you touch it hard.
Lucy hit the ball as hard as she could.

If you **bang** something, you hit it noisily.
Someone banged on the door.

To **beat** can mean to keep hitting with a stick.
Sam beat a red drum.

If something **crashes**, it falls or hits something else with a loud noise.
The whole pile of plates crashed to the floor.

If you **knock** or **bump** something, you hit it hard against something.
She first knocked her head on the cupboard door, and then bumped her knee when she fell over.

To **strike** means the same as to hit.
Let's hope the lightning doesn't strike the house.

To **tap** means to hit a person or thing quickly and lightly.
Miki tapped Jake on the shoulder.

To **slap** or **smack** means to hit someone with the palm of the hand or with something flat.

hole

A **hole** is a gap or opening in something.

These are **some different kinds of holes**.

A **cave** is a big hole under the ground or inside a mountain.

A **burrow** is a hole dug by a rabbit or fox.

A **gap** is a space between things.
Quick, through that gap in the hedge!

A **tear** is a hole or split in a piece of clothing.

A **tunnel** is a long hole under the ground or through a hill.

hot

A
B
C
D
E
F
G
H
I
J
K
L
M
N
O
P
Q
R
S
T
U
V
W
X
Y
Z

When something is **hot**, it burns if you touch it.
Careful, that pan is hot!

If something is **warm**, it is quite hot.
Lucy loves her cosy warm bed.

If you feel **hot**, you are too warm.
Jake felt hot and thirsty.

These words mean very hot.
baking   blazing   boiling   burning   scorching   sweltering

The opposite of **hot** is **cold**.

When you **hurt** part of your body, you feel pain.

If part of your body **aches**, it goes on hurting.

Something that is **sore** feels painful.

Bees and wasps can **sting** you.

A **bruise** is a dark mark on your skin where you have been hit or bumped yourself.

A **burn** is a sore place on your skin you get from something hot.

A **graze** is a sore place on your skin you get by rubbing against something.

A B C D E F G H **I** J K L M N O P Q R S T U V W X Y Z

These are all different kinds of insects.

wasp

dragonfly

cricket

bee

butterfly

fly

ladybird

beetle

ant

grasshopper

A **jewel** is a valuable and beautiful stone.

A **diamond** is a very hard jewel that looks like clear glass.

An **emerald** is a green jewel.

A **pearl** is a jewel that looks like a small, shiny, white ball.

A **ruby** is a red jewel.

Crowns often have jewels in them.

Other things have jewels in them too.

You wear a **necklace** round your neck.

You wear a **ring** on your finger.

You wear **earrings** on your ears.

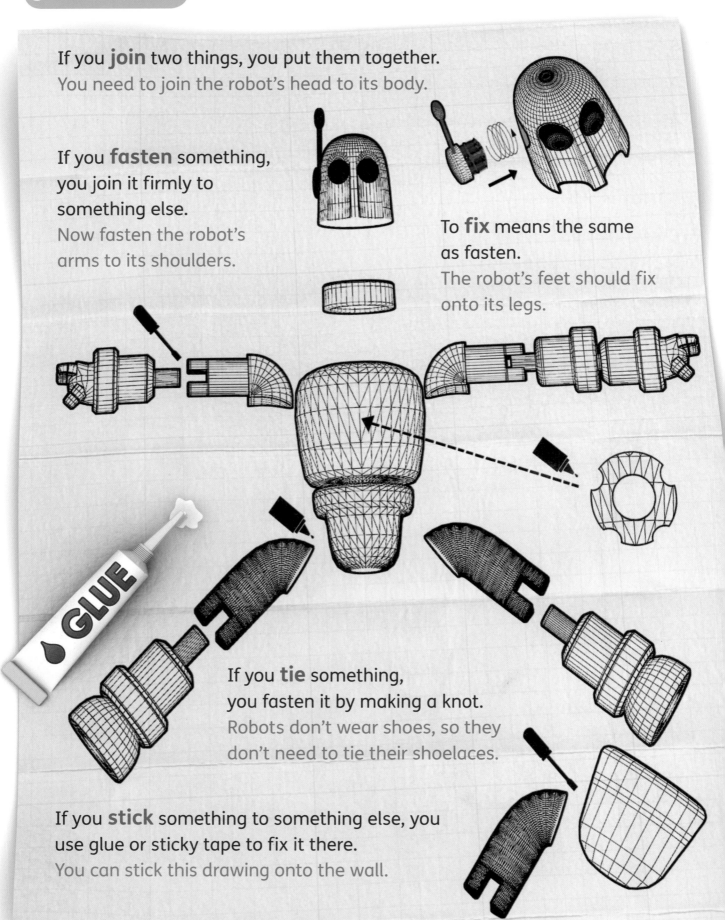

If you **join** two things, you put them together.
You need to join the robot's head to its body.

If you **fasten** something, you join it firmly to something else.
Now fasten the robot's arms to its shoulders.

To **fix** means the same as fasten.
The robot's feet should fix onto its legs.

If you **tie** something, you fasten it by making a knot.
Robots don't wear shoes, so they don't need to tie their shoelaces.

If you **stick** something to something else, you use glue or sticky tape to fix it there.
You can stick this drawing onto the wall.

A B C D E F G H I **J** K L M N O P Q R S T U V W X Y Z

journey

A **journey** is the travelling that people do to get from one place to another.

A **trip** is a short journey.

An **outing** is a trip to somewhere and back again, made for fun.

An **expedition** is a journey made to do something.
We've been on a shopping expedition.

A **voyage** is a journey by ship.

A **drive** is a journey in a car.

A **ride** is a journey on a horse or bicycle.

A **flight** is a journey in an aeroplane.

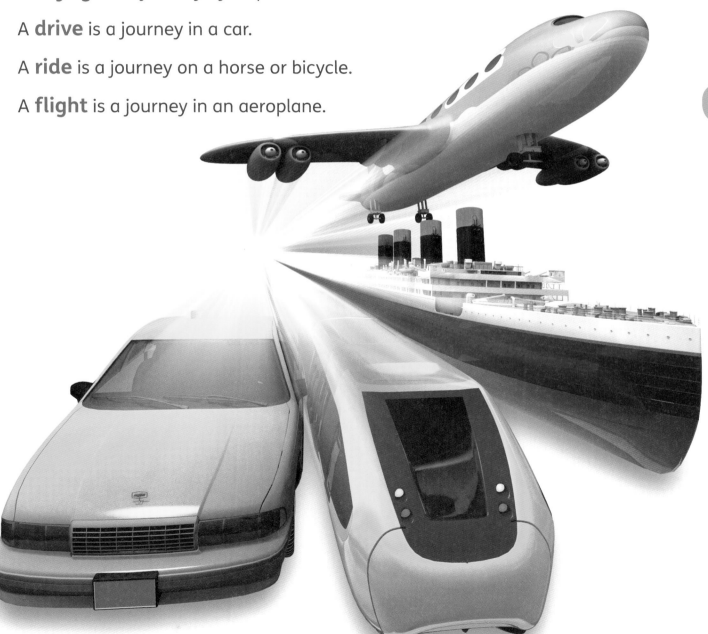

When you **jump**, you go suddenly into the air.
The mouse was jumping up and down in excitement.

Leap means the same as jump.
The horse leaps over the fence.

To **pounce** means to jump on a person or animal suddenly.
Just then the tiger pounced.

When you **hop**, you jump on one foot.
How far can you hop?

When you **skip**, you jump or move along by hopping from one foot to the other.
Lucy skipped along the road.

When you **dive**, you jump head first into water.
Sam dived into the pool.

A B C D E F G H I **J** K L M N O P Q R S T U V W X Y Z

If you **keep** something, you have it as your own and do not give it back or give it away.

Is it all right if I keep one of these photos?

You can also say **have**.

Can I have this photo?

If you **keep** something somewhere, you always put it there.

Sam keeps his toys in the toybox.

If you **save** something, you keep it so that you can use it later.

Jake has been saving up sweet wrappers to make pirate treasure.

If you **store** something, you keep it until it is needed.

Lucy wants to store her trampoline in the garage.

Keep also means to stay as you are.

Keep still! There's a bee on your nose!

If you **stay** somewhere, you do not move away from there.

Stay here and count to twenty.

A
B
C
D
E
F
G
H
I
J
K
L
M
N
O
P
Q
R
S
T
U
V
W
X
Y
Z

When you **know** something, you have found it out and have it in your mind.
Does anyone know the answer?

When you **learn**, you get to know something you did not know before.
We've been learning about space.

When you **remember** something, you bring it back into your mind
when you want to.
Do you remember the name of the biggest planet?

When you **understand** something, you know what it means or how it works.
I don't understand the question about the moon.

laugh

When you **laugh**, you make sounds that show you are happy or think something is funny.

Cackle means to laugh loudly in a nasty way, like a wicked witch does.

Chuckle means to laugh quietly.

Giggle and **titter** mean to laugh in a silly way.

Roar with laughter means to laugh very loudly.

Snigger means to laugh in a quiet, sly way.

light

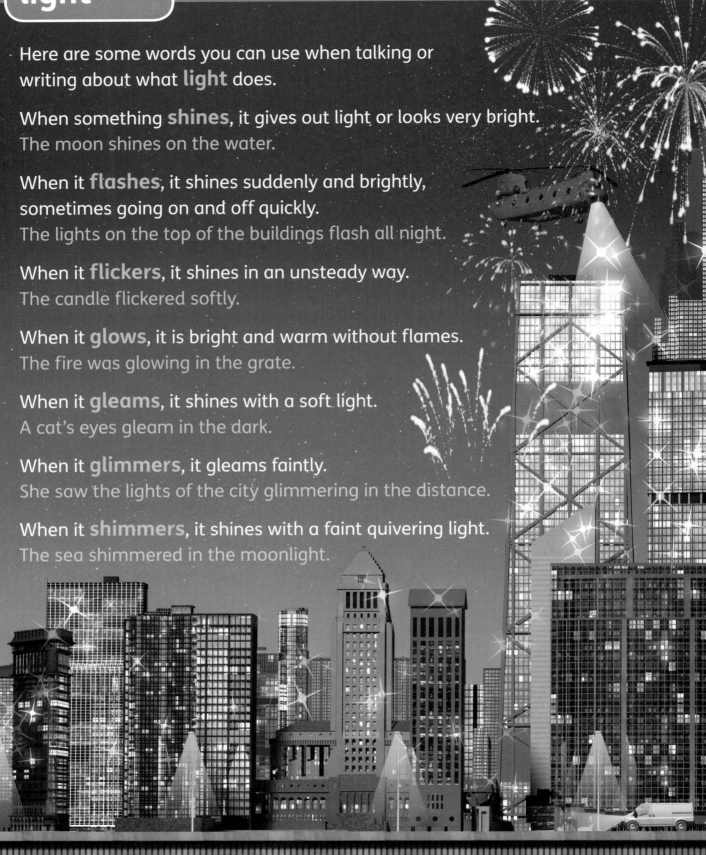

Here are some words you can use when talking or writing about what **light** does.

When something **shines**, it gives out light or looks very bright.
The moon shines on the water.

When it **flashes**, it shines suddenly and brightly, sometimes going on and off quickly.
The lights on the top of the buildings flash all night.

When it **flickers**, it shines in an unsteady way.
The candle flickered softly.

When it **glows**, it is bright and warm without flames.
The fire was glowing in the grate.

When it **gleams**, it shines with a soft light.
A cat's eyes gleam in the dark.

When it **glimmers**, it gleams faintly.
She saw the lights of the city glimmering in the distance.

When it **shimmers**, it shines with a faint quivering light.
The sea shimmered in the moonlight.

light

When it **glistens**, it shines like something wet or polished.
His eyes glistened with tears.

When it **dazzles**, it is so bright that it hurts your eyes.
The car headlights dazzled us.

When it **sparkles**, it shines with a lot of tiny flashes of bright light.
Diamonds sparkled in the candlelight.

When it **glitters**, it sparkles.
Her crown glittered with jewels.

When it **twinkles**, it sparkles.
Twinkle, twinkle, little star.

a
b
c
d
e
f
g
h
i
j
k
l
m
n
o
p
q
r
s
t
u
v
w
x
y
z

If you **like** someone or something, you think it is nice.

Miki likes drawing and painting.

If you **love** someone, you like them very much.

Sam loves his pet cat Oscar.

If you **enjoy** something, you like doing it.

I really enjoy playing football.

If you **want** something, you would like to have it.

Miki wants some paints for her birthday.

If you **feel like** something, you want it.

I feel like an ice cream.

If you **prefer** something, you like it more than something else.

Which do you prefer, the red shirt or the blue shirt?

Your **favourite** is the one you like the most.

Jake's favourite colour is blue, but Lucy's is yellow.

When you **look**, you use your eyes.
Come and look at the parrot.

These are words for different ways of looking.

If you **gaze** at something, you look at it for a long time.
We lay on our backs, gazing at the stars.

If you **glance** at something, you look at it for a very short time.
Oscar glanced down at the mice.

If you **peep** at something, you look at it quickly or secretly.
Sam peeped over the fence.

If you **stare** at something, you look at it for a time without moving your eyes.
It's rude to stare at people.

If you **watch** something, you look at it for a while.
The parrot watched Sam for ages.

A **bunch** is a lot of flowers tied together.

A **bundle** is a lot of sticks tied together.

A **crowd** is a lot of people in one place.

A **queue** is a lot of people in a line.

A **flock** is a lot of birds or sheep.

A **herd** is a lot of cows.

A **shoal** is a lot of fish.

loud

Something that is **loud** makes a lot of sound and is easy to hear.
The music is too loud.

A **noise** is a loud sound.
What is that noise?

A lot of loud sound is **noisy**.
The room was full of noisy children.

You can say that a lot of loud noise is a **din** or a **racket**.
Stop all that din!

Here are some other words for loud noises.

A **bang** is a sudden loud noise.

A **crash** is a very loud noise you hear when something falls or breaks.

A **roar** is the loud sound that a lion makes.

a
b
c
d
e
f
g
h
i
j
k
l
m
n
o
p
q
r
s
t
u
v
w
x
y
z

The opposite of **loud** is **quiet**.

make makes / making / made

To **make** means to get something new by putting other things together.
It took us all week to make the robot.

If you **build** something, you make it by putting parts together.
This summer we are going to build a tree house.

If people **form** a shape, they sit or stand in that shape.
Now let's form a circle.

Make has a lot of other different meanings.

You can often use another word instead.

Uncle Jim wants to make a little speech.
You could say **give** instead.

See if you can make the N into an M.
You could say **turn** or **change** instead.

Four and seven makes eleven.
You could say **adds up to** or **equals** instead.

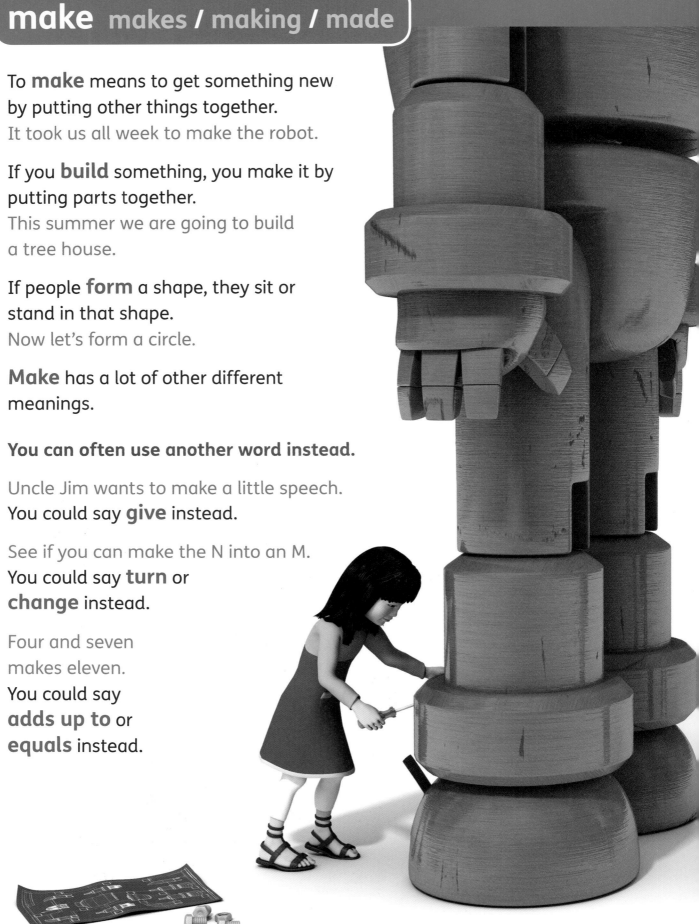
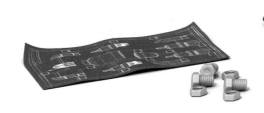

If something you do is **mean** it is not kind to someone else.
Lucy, that was a mean trick!

Unkind means the same thing.

Someone who is **nasty** is not at all kind.

Someone who is **spiteful** says or does horrid things to upset people.

Someone who is **cruel** enjoys hurting people or animals.
The king was a wicked and cruel ruler.

Someone who is **mean** does not like spending money or sharing things.
Uncle Ebenezer was rich but very mean.

Someone who is **selfish** thinks only about themselves and does not share things with other people.
Eating all the ice cream was a selfish thing to do.

a
b
c
d
e
f
g
h
i
j
k
l
m
n
o
p
q
r
s
t
u
v
w
x
y
z

A
B
C
D
E
F
G
H
I
J
K
L
M
N
O
P
Q
R
S
T
U
V
W
X
Y
Z

When you **mix** things, you stir or shake them until they become one thing.
You can make green by mixing blue and yellow.

When you **stir** something, you mix it by moving it round and round with a spoon.
Lucy was busy stirring the paint.

If things are **jumbled up** or **muddled up**, they are mixed up so that they are all in the wrong order.
All Lucy's clothes were jumbled up on the floor.

If you **shuffle** cards, you mix them up before you hand them out.

A **mixture** is made of different things mixed together.
Now pour the cake mixture into a tin.

move

There are many different ways that a person, animal, or thing can move. Here are some of them.

crawl   creep   drop   fall   float   rise

sink   slide   spin   turn   wave   zoom

run

swoop

hover

climb

shake

slither

A
B
C
D
E
F
G
H
I
J
K
L
M
N
O
P
Q
R
S
T
U
V
W
X
Y
Z

Nice is a very common word and it has a lot of different meanings.

You can often use another word instead.

The family next door are very nice.
You could say **friendly** instead.

It was nice of you to bring me a present.
You could say **kind** or **good** or **thoughtful** instead.

Did you have a nice time?
You could say **enjoyable** or **pleasant** instead.

It's a nice day today.
You could say **fine** or **lovely** or **sunny** instead.

You look very nice in that hat.
You could say **pretty** or **handsome** instead.

This cake is nice.
You could say **delicious** or **tasty** instead.

Someone who is **old** has lived for a long time. Something that is **old** was made a long time ago.

Something that is **ancient** is very old.

Prehistoric times were times long ago.

Something that is **shabby** or **tatty** is old and torn.

Something that is **worn out** is so old that you cannot use it any more.

Akjdf didf sikdifik sdifndi vxcelk werlek i fgkifg Imsgfil fg sldikn sdifikn lsdnf
sdifb ksdifib kjfjb d'ejfib dif df 50,000,000 vcxwn xcjd ldm ds ddn

a
b
c
d
e
f
g
h
i
j
k
l
m
n
o
p
q
r
s
t
u
v
w
x
y
z

73

pick

If you **pick** someone or something,
you make up your mind which one you want.

The king picked his bravest knight to fight the dragon.

Choose means the same as pick.

Sam and Jake are choosing the sweets they want.

If you **pick** flowers, fruit, or vegetables,
you take them from where they are growing.

The princess picked some flowers.

If you **gather** them, you collect them together from different places.

Let's gather all the apples that have fallen from the trees.

These are different kinds of pictures.

A **drawing** is something you draw with a pencil or crayon.

A **painting** is a picture that someone has painted.

A **portrait** is a picture of a person.

A **photo** is a picture taken with a camera.

A **cartoon** is a drawing that tells a joke.

A **map** is a drawing of part of the world.

A **poster** is a large picture or notice for everyone to see.

a
b
c
d
e
f
g
h
i
j
k
l
m
n
o
p
q
r
s
t
u
v
w
x
y
z

pull

If you **pull** something, you get hold of it and make it come towards you.
The mice pulled hard on the ropes.

If you **drag** something, you pull it along the ground.
They slowly dragged the heavy box across the floor.

If you **tug** something, you pull it hard.
Stop tugging my arm!

If you **tow** a car or boat, you pull it behind you.
They towed our car to the garage.

If you **stretch** something, you pull it to make it longer, wider, or tighter.
The washing line was stretched tight.

If you **draw** curtains, you pull them to open them or close them.

When you **push** something, you use your hands to move it away from you.
Oscar helped the mice push the box across the floor.

When you **press** something, you push hard on it.
Sam pressed the red button to see what would happen.

If you **shove** something, you push it hard.
The crowd pushed and shoved.

If you **poke** something or someone, you push them hard with a stick or your finger.
The baby just poked me in the eye!

If you **nudge** someone, you push them with your elbow.
I nudged my sister and pointed to the frog under the table.

If you **stick** something sharp into a thing, you push the point in.
What happens if you stick a pin in a balloon?

a
b
c
d
e
f
g
h
i
j
k
l
m
n
o
p
q
r
s
t
u
v
w
x
y
z

A
B
C
D
E
F
G
H
I
J
K
L
M
N
O
P
Q
R
S
T
U
V
W
X
Y
Z

If you **put** something in a place, you move it there.

Where did you put the scissors?

You can use these different words to talk about putting things somewhere.

If you **leave** something somewhere, you let it stay where it is.

You can leave your bag here.

If you **place** something somewhere, you put it there carefully.

Miki placed the last brick on the top.

If you **lay** something somewhere, you put it down carefully.

Now lay the cloth on the table.

If you **arrange** things, you put them in order or make them look tidy.

Lucy arranged the books on the shelf.

If you **pile** things, you put a number of them on top of one another.

Miki piled up the bricks into a tower.

If you **hang** something, you fix the top of it to a hook or nail.

Hang your coat on one of the hooks.

quiet

If someone or something is **quiet**,
they make very little noise, or no noise at all.
The mice tried to be as quiet as possible.

If someone or something is **silent**,
they do not talk or make a sound at all.
Everyone was silent when the queen walked in.

Soft means gentle and quiet.
We could hear soft music.

Here are some other words for quiet sounds.

To **hum** means to make a low sound like a bee.

To **murmur** means to speak softly.

To **patter** means to make light tapping sounds.

To **purr** means to make a gentle murmuring
sound like a cat when it is pleased.

To **rustle** means to make a gentle sound
like dry leaves being blown by the wind.

To **tick** means to make the sound of
a watch or clock.

To **whisper** means to speak very softly.

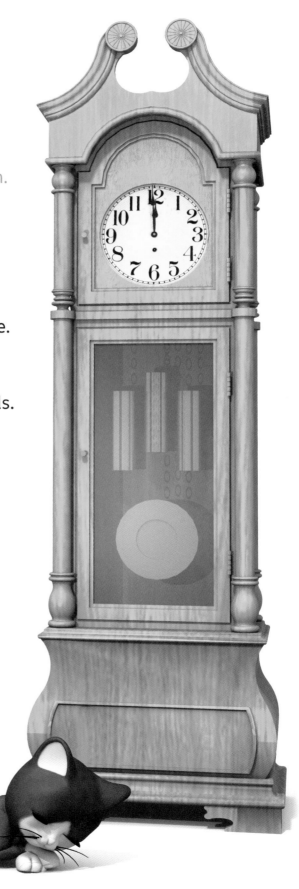

The opposite of **quiet** is **loud**.

A
B
C
D
E
F
G
H
I
J
K
L
M
N
O
P
Q
R
S
T
U
V
W
X
Y
Z

When you **run**, you use your legs to move quickly.

Here are some other words that mean run.

To **dash** means to run because you are in a hurry.
Jake dashed out of the door.

Rush means the same as dash.
Lucy rushed downstairs to answer the phone.

If people **race**, they have a contest to find out who is the fastest.

To **scamper** means to run quickly.
Rabbits scamper to their burrows.

To **scurry** means to run with short steps.
The mice scurried across the ground.

When a horse **gallops**, it runs as fast as it can.

When a horse **trots**, it runs quite slowly.

safe

If someone is **safe**, they are free from danger.
All the birds felt safe in the tree.

To **protect** someone or something
means to keep them safe.
The pigeons protected their nest from the cat.

Something that is **safe** is not dangerous.
Is that ladder safe?

Harmless means safe to be near.
Don't worry, Oscar the cat is harmless.

Tame animals are not wild
or dangerous.
These mice are very tame,
aren't they?

To **save** means to free someone
or something from danger.
Do you think the birds
need saving from Oscar?

Rescue means the
same as save.
The fire brigade once had
to rescue Oscar from a tree.

a
b
c
d
e
f
g
h
i
j
k
l
m
n
o
p
q
r
s
t
u
v
w
x
y
z

81

A B C D E F G H I J K L M N O P Q R **S** T U V W X Y Z

When you **say** something, you use your voice to make words.
What did you say?

When you **speak**, you say something.
Could you speak more slowly?

When you **talk**, you speak to other people.
Miki talked to her friend Jake.

When you **ask** something, you put a question to someone or say that you want something.

When you **reply**, you give an answer.
'Can we go to the park?' Jake asked.
'In a little while,' his mother replied.

When you **answer**, you speak when someone calls you or asks you a question.
'Do you want to know a secret?' Lucy asked.
'Yes,' Sam answered.

When you **tell** a person something, you pass on a story, news, or instructions.
Sam is good at telling jokes.

When you **whisper**, you speak very softly.

When you **mumble**, you speak so that you are not easy to hear.

When you **shout**, you speak very loudly.

When you **see**,
you use your eyes to get to know something.
How many mice can you see?

If you **notice** something, you see it and think about it.
Did you notice the egg?

If you **spot** something, you notice it.
Can you spot the ball?

If you **glimpse** something, you see it for only a very short time.
I glimpsed a castle through the trees.

If you **watch** something, you look to see what happens.
We watched Jake juggling all sorts of things.

a
b
c
d
e
f
g
h
i
j
k
l
m
n
o
p
q
r
S
t
u
v
w
x
y
z

shake shakes / shaking / shook / shaken

When a thing **shakes**, it moves quickly up and down or from side to side.

If you **shiver** or **shudder**, you shake because you are cold or frightened.

If a person or animal **trembles**, they shake gently, especially because they are frightened.

Quiver and **quake** mean the same as tremble.

If a person or thing **wobbles**, they move in an unsteady way from side to side.
Look, Miki is starting to wobble.

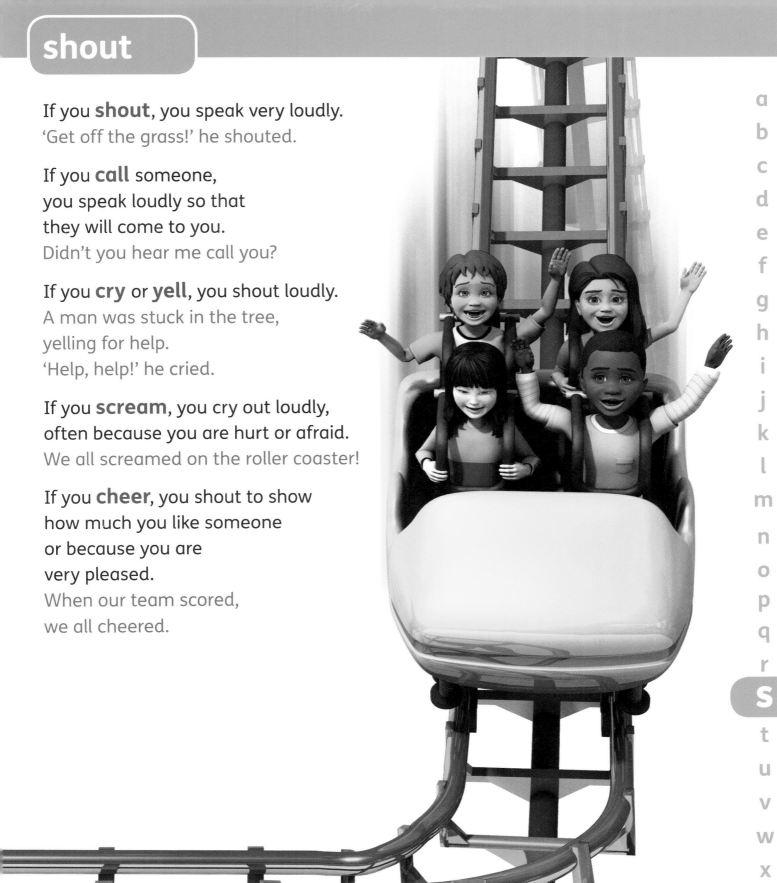

If you **shout**, you speak very loudly.
'Get off the grass!' he shouted.

If you **call** someone,
you speak loudly so that
they will come to you.
Didn't you hear me call you?

If you **cry** or **yell**, you shout loudly.
A man was stuck in the tree,
yelling for help.
'Help, help!' he cried.

If you **scream**, you cry out loudly,
often because you are hurt or afraid.
We all screamed on the roller coaster!

If you **cheer**, you shout to show
how much you like someone
or because you are
very pleased.
When our team scored,
we all cheered.

a
b
c
d
e
f
g
h
i
j
k
l
m
n
o
p
q
r
S
t
u
v
w
x
y
z

A
B
C
D
E
F
G
H
I
J
K
L
M
N
O
P
Q
R
S
T
U
V
W
X
Y
Z

If someone **shows** you how to do something, they do it so that you can watch them.
Lucy showed me how to make a cake.

When someone **teaches** you to do something, they show you how to do it.
My dad is teaching me to ride a bike.

When someone **explains** something, they make it clear so that people will understand it.
I'll explain the rules of the game.

When someone **tells** you how to do something, they give you the information you need to do it.
These instructions tell you how to make a birthday cake.

When you **show** something, you let it be seen.
Show me your new bike.

If you **display** something, you show it.
The latest games are displayed in the shop window.

When you **point**, you show where something is by holding out your finger towards it.
Point to the lolly you want.

1.
2.
3.
4.
5.

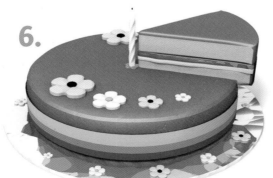

6.

shut shuts / shutting / shut

To **shut** means to move a cover, lid, or door to block an opening.

Have you shut the door?

To **close** means the same as to shut.

If you **slam** a door, you shut it loudly.

If you **fasten** something, you close it or do it up.

Don't forget to fasten the gate behind you.

If you **lock** a door or lid, you fasten it so it cannot be opened without a key.

sleep sleeps / sleeping / slept

When you **sleep**, you close your eyes and your body rests as you do every night.

When you are **asleep**, you are sleeping.

These words are all to do with sleeping.

If you are **sleepy** or **tired**, you want to go to sleep.

To **drop off** or **nod off** means to go to sleep.

To **doze** means to sleep lightly.

To **take a nap** means to have a short sleep.

When you **dream**, you see and hear things in your sleep.

If someone **snores**, they breathe very noisily while they are sleeping.

When you have finished sleeping, you **wake up**.

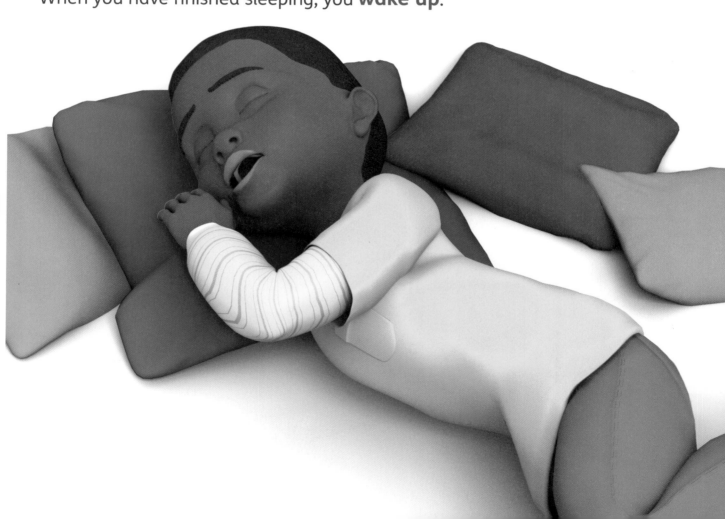

To **slide** means to move smoothly
over something slippery or polished.
People were sliding on the ice.

You can **skate** on ice too.
We went skating at the ice rink.

If a car **skids**, it slides without meaning to.

If you **slip**, you slide suddenly without meaning to.
The clown slipped on a banana skin.

If something **slithers**, it slides as it moves along.
A snake slithered along the ground.

a
b
c
d
e
f
g
h
i
j
k
l
m
n
o
p
q
r
s
t
u
v
w
x
y
z

89

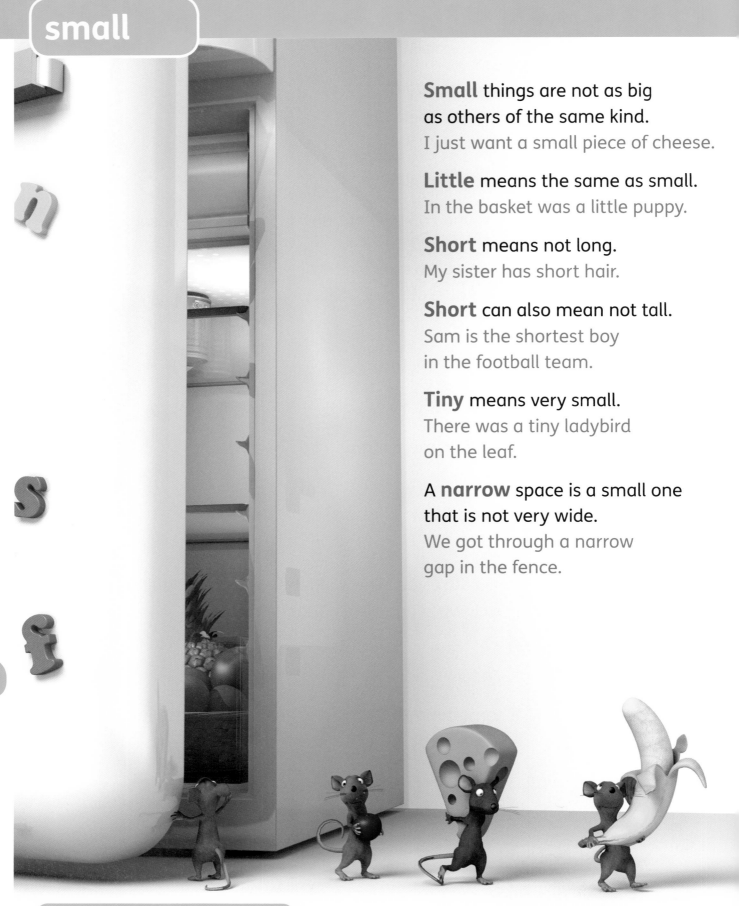

small

A B C D E F G H I J K L M N O P Q R **S** T U V W X Y Z

Small things are not as big as others of the same kind.
I just want a small piece of cheese.

Little means the same as small.
In the basket was a little puppy.

Short means not long.
My sister has short hair.

Short can also mean not tall.
Sam is the shortest boy in the football team.

Tiny means very small.
There was a tiny ladybird on the leaf.

A **narrow** space is a small one that is not very wide.
We got through a narrow gap in the fence.

The opposite of **small** is **big**.

When you **smell** something, you use your nose to find out about it.
Can you smell Miki's flower?

If you **sniff** something, you smell it.
The dog sniffed happily at the leaves.

When something **smells**, you can find out about it with your nose.
Your socks smell awful.

Perfume is a liquid with a nice sweet smell.

A **scent** is a perfume.

A **scent** is also an animal's smell, that other animals can follow.

A **stink** or **pong** is a nasty smell.

You can say that something with a nasty smell is **smelly**.

a
b
c
d
e
f
g
h
i
j
k
l
m
n
o
p
q
r
s
t
u
v
w
x
y
z

soft

Things that are **soft** are not hard or firm.
Lucy loves her soft teddy.

Something that is **fluffy** has soft hair, fur, or feathers.
A fluffy yellow chick hopped out.

Something that is **floppy** is soft and not stiff.
Miki was wearing a floppy hat.

Something that is **squashy** is easy to press out of shape.
This banana has gone squashy.

The opposite of **soft** is **hard**.

sound

A **sound** is anything that can be heard.

A **noise** is a loud sound.

bang

bleep

bubble

buzz

clang

click

crackle

crunch

drip

fizz

plop

rattle

ring

rumble

splash

tick

toot

whirr

whistle

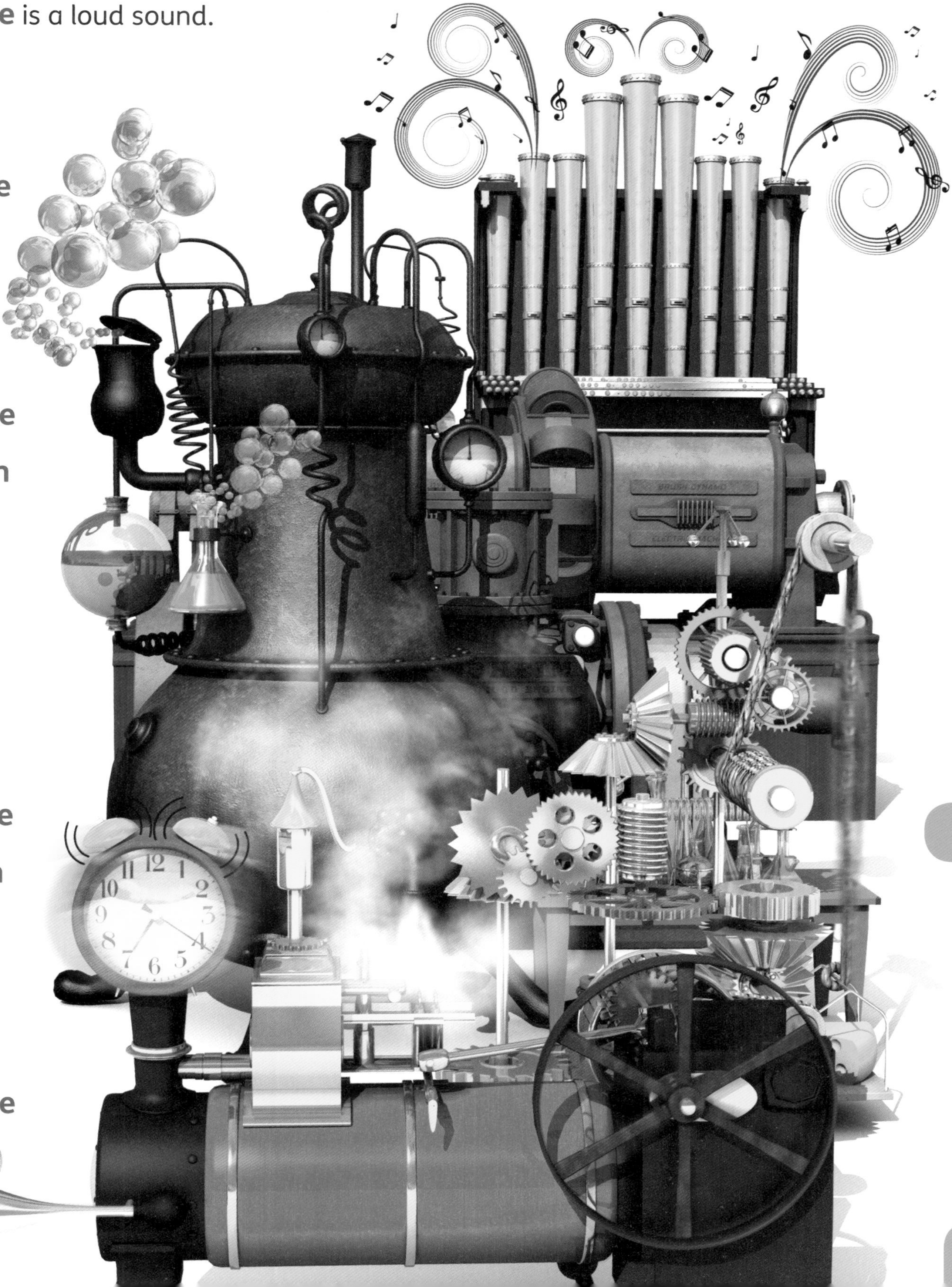

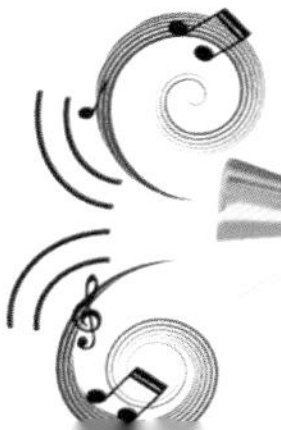

A
B
C
D
E
F
G
H
I
J
K
L
M
N
O
P
Q
R
S
T
U
V
W
X
Y
Z

Space is everything beyond the earth, where the stars and planets are. Here are some words you can use if you are talking or writing about space.

A **spacecraft** or **spaceship** is a machine that can carry people and things through space.

An **astronaut** is a person who travels in a spacecraft.

An astronaut wears a **spacesuit**.

A **space station** is a kind of spacecraft that stays in space. People live on it for a time to do experiments to find out about space.

The **stars** are the tiny, bright lights you see in the sky at night.

space station

planet

spaceship

astronaut

space

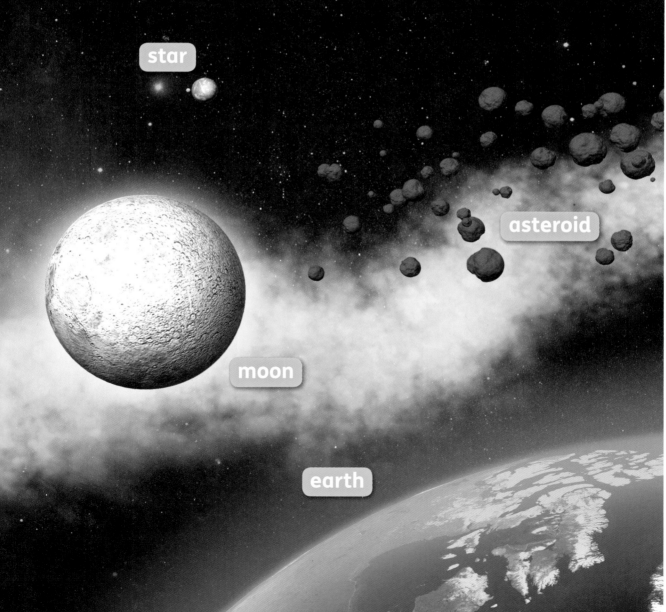

The **sun** gives the earth heat and light.
It is a star, and the earth moves round it.

A **planet** is any of the worlds in space that move around a star.

Earth is the planet that we live on.

The **moon** moves around the earth once every twenty-eight days.
You can often see the moon in the sky at night.

Asteroids are very small planets that move around the sun.

sun

star

asteroid

moon

earth

When you **start**, you take the first steps in doing something.
Miki is just about to start.

When you **begin**,
you start something.
Sam is beginning to
catch Lucy up.

If you **set out** or **set off**, you start a journey.
One of the mice is waving as she sets off across the road.
The opposite of **start** is **stop** or **end** or **finish**.

If a person or thing **stops** doing something, they do not do it any more.
Stop waving, Jake – you'll fall off!

When you **finish**, you come to the end of something.
Jake is the first to finish.

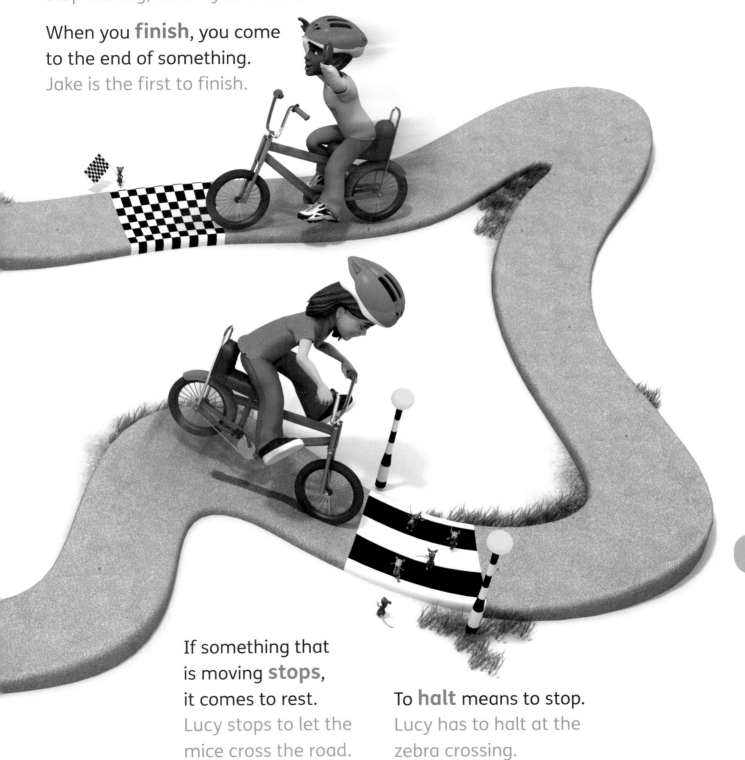

If something that is moving **stops**, it comes to rest.
Lucy stops to let the mice cross the road.

To **halt** means to stop.
Lucy has to halt at the zebra crossing.

The opposite of **stop** is **start**.

A **story** tells you something that has happened. Stories can be made up, or they can be about real things.

An old word for a story is **tale**.

A **fairy tale** is a story in which magic things happen.

A **legend** is an old story that has been handed down from the past.

An **adventure** is an exciting story.

You can **tell** a story, or **read** it, or **listen** to it. The storyteller began to tell his tale.

strange

If something is **strange**, it is not like anything you have seen or heard before.
A strange creature came out of the box.

If something is **unusual** or **odd**, it seems strange.
What an odd name!

Something **funny** seems strange.
There's a funny smell in the kitchen.

These words also mean strange.

extraordinary

peculiar

curious

strong

A
B
C
D
E
F
G
H
I
J
K
L
M
N
O
P
Q
R
S
T
U
V
W
X
Y
Z

Strong people or animals are healthy and can carry heavy things and work hard.
The elephant was strong enough to carry three logs.

Mighty and **powerful** mean very strong.
He gave a mighty blow with his hammer.

Something **strong** is hard to break or damage.
We tied the boat with a strong rope.

If something is strong and will last a long time, you can say that it is **tough** or **sturdy**.
Jake has a new pair of tough yellow boots.

If you are **sure** about something, you know it is true or right.

'I'm sure I locked the elephant's cage,' thought the zookeeper.

Certain means the same as sure.

Are you certain you know the right answer?

Positive means the same as sure.

I am positive that my money was in my coat pocket.

If you are sure something happened or will happen, you can say that it **definitely** or **certainly** happened or will happen.

Yes, I definitely locked the cage door.

surprise

A **surprise** is something that you did not expect.
What a lovely surprise!

If something **surprises** you, it is something that you did not expect.

If something **shocks** you, it gives you a sudden nasty surprise.

If something **amazes** or **astonishes** or **astounds** you,
it surprises you very much.
Miki was astonished to see a puppet jumping out of the box.

If you **take** something to a place, you have it with you when you go there.
Everyone took presents to the party.
You can also say **bring**.

If you **carry** something, you hold it and take it from one place to another.
Miki was carrying a colourful umbrella.

When you **take** something, you get it in your hands.
Take a biscuit from the jar.

If you **hold** something, you have it in your hands or arms.
Lucy was holding a bunch of flowers.

When you **catch** something that is moving, you get hold of it.
I'll throw the ball and you catch it.

If you **grab** something, you take hold of it quickly or roughly.
The thief grabbed the bag and ran off.

a
b
c
d
e
f
g
h
i
j
k
l
m
n
o
p
q
r
s
t
u
v
w
x
y
z

A
B
C
D
E
F
G
H
I
J
K
L
M
N
O
P
Q
R
S
T
U
V
W
X
Y
Z

When you **talk**, you speak to other people.

Don't interrupt while I'm talking.

If you **chat** with someone, you have a friendly talk with them.

I chatted with our neighbour.

If you **chatter**, you talk too quickly or too much.

Sam is always chattering in class.

When people **discuss** things, they talk about them.

We've been discussing the best way to make a robot.

When people **argue**, they talk about things they do not agree on.

If people **gossip**, they talk a lot about other people.

taste

The **taste** of something is what it is like when you eat or drink it.
I don't like the taste of cheese.

A **flavour** is a type of taste.
What flavour of crisps do you want?

If something tastes nice, you can say that it is **delicious** or **tasty**.
This ice cream is delicious.

Here are some different kinds of taste.

Sugar and honey have a **sweet** taste.

Lemons have a **sour** taste.

Curry has a **hot** and **spicy** taste.

tell tells / telling / told

A
B
C
D
E
F
G
H
I
J
K
L
M
N
O
P
Q
R
S
T
U
V
W
X
Y
Z

If someone **tells** you something, they pass on news or instructions or a story.

The storyteller began to tell his tale.

When someone **explains** something, they make it clear so that people will understand it.

Lucy explained the rules of the game to Jake.

When you **promise**, you say you will really do or not do something.

You promised we could go swimming.

If you **warn** someone, you tell them that there is danger.

Dad warned us not to go too near the river.

If you **announce** something, you tell everyone about it.

At assembly, Mrs Doyle announced that she would leave at the end of term.

If someone **tells** you to do something, they say you must do it.

Sam told his dog to pick the ball up.

If someone **orders** you to do something, they tell you to do it.

The king ordered his men to enter the forest.

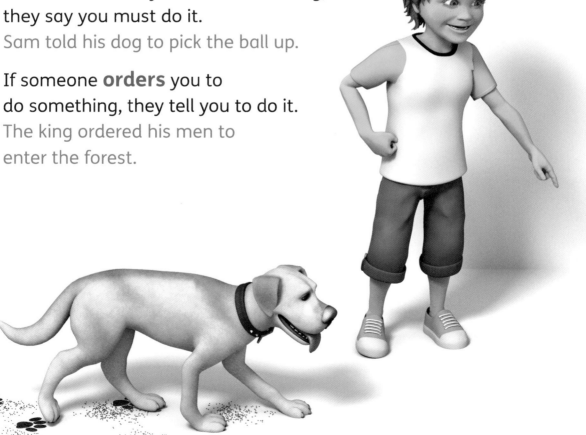

thin

Something that is **thin** does not measure much from one side to the other.
Giraffes have long thin necks and long thin legs.

Narrow means the same as thin.
A narrow path leads through the forest.

A **thin** person does not have much fat on their body.
Uncle Alex is tall and thin.

Slim and **slender** both mean thin and graceful.

You can also say that a thin person is **lean**.

a
b
c
d
e
f
g
h
i
j
k
l
m
n
o
p
q
r
s
t
u
v
w
x
y
z

When you **think**, you use your mind.
Can you think of the answer?

If you **think** something, you have an idea or opinion.
I think we should go now.

Here are some other words to do with thinking.

If you **concentrate**, you think hard about something.
Be quiet, I'm trying to concentrate.

If you **believe** something, you feel sure it is true or real.
Do you believe in ghosts?

If you **expect** something, you think it is very likely to happen.
I expect there will be lots of people in the park.

If you **imagine** something, you make a picture of it in your mind.
Imagine you are a brave knight.

If you **remember** something, you bring it back into your mind when you want to.
I can't remember her name.

A
B
C
D
E
F
G
H
I
J
K
L
M
N
O
P
Q
R
S
T
U
V
W
X
Y
Z

throw throws / throwing / threw / thrown

When you **throw** something, you make it leave your hand and move through the air.
Miki threw three things. Which went the furthest?

If you **toss** something, you throw it somewhere.
We tossed some bread to the ducks.

If you **fling** something, you throw it without being careful about it.
Lucy ran into her room, flinging her coat onto the bed.

A
B
C
D
E
F
G
H
I
J
K
L
M
N
O
P
Q
R
S
T
U
V
W
X
Y
Z

If you **touch** something, you put your fingers on it.

My knee is sore, so don't touch it.

If you **feel** something, you touch it to find out what it is like.

I can feel a bump on my head.

These are words for different ways of touching a person or thing.

If you **cuddle** someone you love, you put your arms closely round them.

If you **kiss** someone, you touch them with your lips.

If you **pat** something, you tap it gently with your hand.

If you can **reach** something, you can stretch out to touch it.

touch

If you **rub** something, you press your hand on it and move it backwards and forwards.

If you **scratch**, you rub your fingernails over your skin because it itches.

If you **stroke** something, you move your hand gently along it.

If you **tickle** someone, you keep touching their skin lightly so that you make them laugh.

Here are some words you can use to say what something is like when you touch it.

soft   hard   prickly   furry

smooth   rough   wet   dry

lumpy   slimy   hot   cold

A
B
C
D
E
F
G
H
I
J
K
L
M
N
O
P
Q
R
S
T
U
V
W
X
Y
Z

When something **turns**, it moves round.
All the different wheels began to turn.

To **spin** means to turn round and round quickly.
Let's spin a coin to see who starts.

To **twirl** means to turn round and round quickly.
She twirled round as she danced.

When you **twist** or **screw** something,
you turn it round so that you can
take it off or put it on.
You need to twist the lid off.

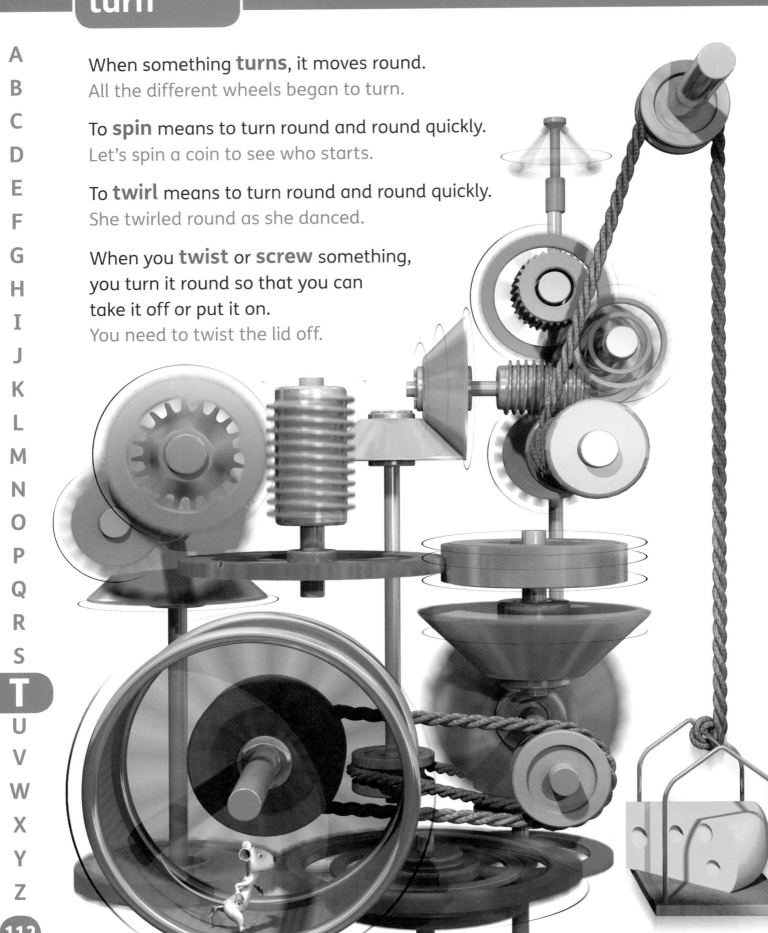

unhappy

If you are **unhappy**, you are not happy.

Sad means the same as unhappy.

You can also use these other words.

glum Why are you looking so glum?

heartbroken Sam was heartbroken when he thought his cat Oscar was lost.

upset There's no need to get upset. We can mend your teddy.

If you are **disappointed**, you feel sad because something you were hoping for did not happen. We are disappointed that we lost the game.

The opposite of **unhappy** or **sad** is **happy**.

These are all different kinds of vegetables.

aubergine

beans

cabbage

carrots

cauliflower

courgettes

onions

parsnip

peas

potatoes

spinach

yams

walk

When you **walk**, you move along by putting one foot in front of the other.

You can use these words to talk about different ways of walking.

If you **stride**, you walk with long steps.

If you **march**, you walk like a soldier, with regular steps.

If you **tiptoe**, you walk on your toes very quietly or carefully.

If you **creep** somewhere, you walk very slowly and quietly so no one will hear you.

If you **limp**, you walk with difficulty because there is something wrong with your leg or foot.

If you **stagger**, you walk in an unsteady way as if you are just about to fall.

A
B
C
D
E
F
G
H
I
J
K
L
M
N
O
P
Q
R
S
T
U
V
W
X
Y
Z

Here are some words you can use when talking or writing about how water moves.

When water **flows**, it moves along like a river.
The stream flows very fast here.

When it **pours**, it flows downwards quickly.
Rainwater poured off the roof.

When it **splashes**, it flies about in drops.
The water splashed all over me.

When it **sprays**, it scatters in tiny drops.
The car drove through the puddle and sprayed us with water.

When it **laps**, it makes a gentle splash.
Small waves were lapping against the rocks.

When it **gushes**, it flows quickly.
Water gushed out of the burst pipe.

When it **squirts**, it comes out in a thin fast jet.
One of the mice is squirting water over the others.

When it **drips**, it falls in drops.
Can you hear that dripping tap?

When it **trickles**, it flows slowly
in small amounts.
Tears trickled down her face.

a
b
c
d
e
f
g
h
i
j
k
l
m
n
o
p
q
r
s
t
u
v
w
x
y
z

These are all different kinds of weather.

cloud   gale   hail   ice   lightning   rain   shower

snow   storm   sunshine   thunder   wind

wet

If something is **wet**, it is covered in water, or it has water in it.

These words mean very wet.

soaked Miki and Oscar got completely soaked in the rain.

soggy The ground is very soggy.

These words mean slightly wet.

damp The coats are still damp.

moist Keep the soil moist to help the seeds grow.

The opposite of **wet** is **dry.**

A B C D E F G H I J K L M N O P Q R S T U V **W** X Y Z

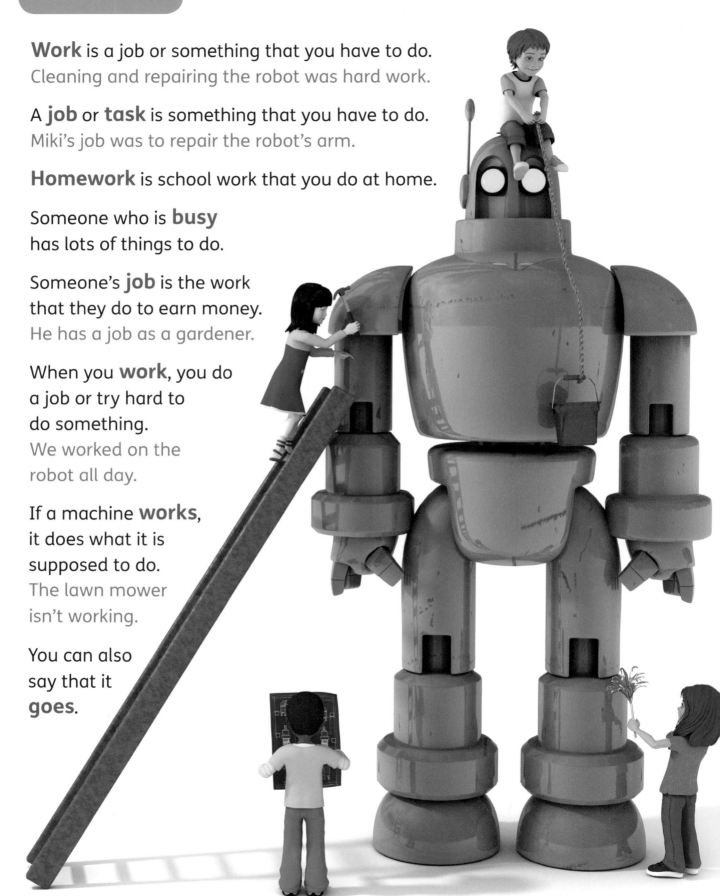

Work is a job or something that you have to do.
Cleaning and repairing the robot was hard work.

A **job** or **task** is something that you have to do.
Miki's job was to repair the robot's arm.

Homework is school work that you do at home.

Someone who is **busy** has lots of things to do.

Someone's **job** is the work that they do to earn money.
He has a job as a gardener.

When you **work**, you do a job or try hard to do something.
We worked on the robot all day.

If a machine **works**, it does what it is supposed to do.
The lawn mower isn't working.

You can also say that it **goes**.

X

We put **X** to show where something is, especially on a map.

X marks the spot.

This is also called a **cross**.

Pirate Jake has put a cross on the map to show where the treasure is.

young

A person or animal that is **young** was born not long ago.

These are words for young people.

A **baby** is a very young child.

A **child** is a young boy or girl.

A **boy** is a male child or young adult.

A **girl** is a female child or young adult.

These are words for young animals.

A **calf** is a young cow.

A **foal** is a young horse.

A **kid** is a young goat.

A **lamb** is a young sheep.

A **chick** is a baby bird.

A **cub** is a young lion, tiger, fox, or bear.

A **duckling** is a young duck.

A **joey** is a young kangaroo.

A **kitten** is a young cat.

A **puppy** is a young dog.

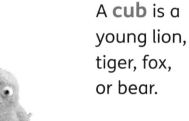

The opposite of **young** is **old**.

zoom

To **zoom** means to move along very quickly.

Other words that mean the same are

hurtle   race   speed   streak   whizz

Index

Index

Index

Index

Index